# THE NEGRO
# SINGS A NEW HEAVEN

# BLACK REDISCOVERY
### A SERIES EDITED BY PHILIP S. FONER
#### Professor of History, Lincoln University

# THE NEGRO
# SINGS A NEW HEAVEN

By

MARY ALLEN GRISSOM

DOVER PUBLICATIONS, INC., NEW YORK

784.756
GRI

Published in Canada by General Publishing Company, Ltd.,
30 Lesmill Road, Don Mills, Toronto, Ontario.
Published in the United Kingdom by Constable and Company, Ltd.,
10 Orange Street, London WC 2.


This Dover edition, first published in 1969, is an
unabridged and unaltered republication of the work
first published in 1930 by The University of North
Carolina Press, Chapel Hill.


*Standard Book Number: 486-22458-9*
*Library of Congress Catalog Card Number: 70-92392*

Manufactured in the United States of America
Dover Publications, Inc.
180 Varick Street
New York, N.Y. 10014

# FOREWORD

THESE SONGS constitute a part of collections of original melodies whose value lies in their presentation and preservation exactly as they are found and sung. Thus collected and preserved they provide portraiture of the Negro folk song and background and remain a treasure source for future harmonization if that should be desired. Their chief value, therefore, lies in their simplicity and realism, recording a true emancipation of spirit from child-like irresponsibility to a growing consciousness of citizenship, thus contributing another chapter to the complete record of southern Negro folk songs. Most of the songs included in this volume have been taken directly from the Negroes in their present-day worship, and have been selected from those sung in the neighborhood of Louisville, Kentucky, and certain rural sections in Adair County.

Many of the tunes are led by the older Negroes who are able to add modern verses to the old tunes, making them fit present-day needs, yet losing none of their former setting of dignity and beauty. Herein, lies much of their charm. Others are left just as they were sung years ago. The wonder is that they are handed down from generation to generation with such accuracy. Another group shows a decided influence of the white man's modern Sunday school and revival songs used in the South, but with words of such character as to place them, in sentiment at least, to the credit of the Negro's contribution to original folksong. Most of the songs are best suited to group singing. Some, however, lose none of their beauty when sung by the lone Negro.

The syncopation is never to be exaggerated. It should be thought of rather as strong and weak tones than as long and short ones. Care should be given to the manner of taking hold of the stressed tone—rather pushing to the accent than attacking it with vigor, using lighter tone quality on the unstressed tones. This is indicated by the usual accent marks and also by small lines under certain notes and words to emphasize the thought expressed. Care should be given to smooth "pushing" in order not to render a sharp, ragged, rhythm utterly unlike the subtle irregularities one hears when the Negro is singing. There is also a suggestion of spoken emphasis in many instances where these lines occur.

The Negro's innate feel for a simple, harmonic background for all his melodies would appear largely responsible for the queer sliding manner in which he sings. It has been noted that he does this much more when singing alone than when singing with a group. It is so easy for the Negro to swing from a major to a minor melody or harmony that his music is more often thought of as minor than major, whereas a large percentage of it is definitely major. This may explain the popular theory that he creates unusual harmonies. What he really does is to supply his own harmonic background as he sings his melody. In this volume this is indicated by very small notes with lines leading to and from them to show of which melody tone they are to be the harmonic support. These are rather to be thought than sung, so lightly are they sounded. They are in no sense grace notes. The use of actual cessation of tone, indicated by a comma, is one of the most effective things the Negro does to create interest in his songs. The dialect follows no set rules but is put down as it was heard. It is never uniform, the ending of a word depending upon what follows. Frequently one word may have three pronunciations in the same song, as for example, *my, mah* or *muh* according to what precedes or follows it,—*my,* if much emphasized. These songs conform to the primitive Negro singing which is accompanied by hand clapping and stamping of the feet, each frequently giving a different grouping of the notes to the beat.

The attempt has been made to have the accompanying text follow the same order as the music. For example, the Negro song frequently opens with the chorus, sung in unison by the group. A sort of recitative by the leader follows as the verse, and then the chorus by the group is again taken up. Thus solo and chorus alternate throughout the song which ends with the chorus. In only one or two cases is the chorus repeated in full in the text, and these are instances where the nature of the music demands it. In all other cases, where the sequence is perfectly clear from the music, neither the chorus itself nor the word "chorus" has been inserted between the stanzas.

Too much cannot be said against the tendency to accompany these melodies with elaborate harmonies. The harmony used by them is the simplest, but made unforgettable by counter-melodies hummed while the leader creates his mood. The response comes as the positive dignified and beautiful approval of the religious thought expressed. If the Negro uses unusual chords, it is usually due to the fact that he has heard choral singing by the white people and is attempting to reproduce what he hears. When he creates with his wonderful native impulse, the world is given harmony that is beautiful in its simplicity; rhythm that baffles, but retains a dignity of expression; and melody that ranks high in any standard of creative work.

Acknowledgment is here made to the Institute for Research in Social Science of the University of North Carolina for coöperation and valuable help in the plan of presentation and for making possible the publication of this volume. To Mr. Paul J. Weaver of the University of North Carolina for his critical reading of the text and music and for valuable suggestions, appreciation is expressed. And I am especially indebted to Mr. E. J. Wotawa, of the School of Music of the University of Louisville, for his very excellent copy of the original manuscript and his enthusiastic support throughout the entire period of compilation; and to my many friends for belief and encouragement in the idea of publishing the songs.

M. A. G.

Louisville, Kentucky,
June, 1930.

# TABLE OF CONTENTS

## V. SONGS OF SERVICE AND PERSONAL EXPERIENCE (Cont.)

## VI. SHOUTING SONGS AND SONGS OF TRIUMPH

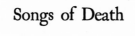

Songs of Death

# THAT LONESOME VALLEY

# THAT LONESOME VALLEY

When you walk-a that lonesome Valley,
You got tuh walk it by yo'sef;
No one heah may walk it with you,
You got tuh walk it by yo'sef.

CHORUS
*Oh you got tuh walk-a that lonesome Valley,*
*You got tuh go tha by yo'sef*
*No one heah to go tha with you,*
*You got tuh go tha by yo'sef.*

When you reach the rivah Jurdun,
You got tuh cross it by yo'sef;
No one heah may cross it with you,
You got tuh cross it by yo'sef.

When you face that Judgmunt mawnin',
You got tuh face it by yo'sef;
No one heah to face it faw you,
You got tuh face it by yo'sef.

Loud an' strong yo Mastuh callin',
You got tuh answer by yo'sef;
No one heah to answer faw you,
You got tuh answer by yo'sef.

You got tuh stand yo' trial in Judgmunt,
You got tuh stand it by yo'sef;
No one heah to stand it faw you,
You got tuh stand it by yo'sef.

Jurdun's stream is cold and chilly,
You got tuh wade it by yo'sef;
No one heah to wade it faw you,
You got tuh wade it by yo'sef.

When my dear Lawd was hangin' bleedin',
He had tuh hang tha by His-sef;
No one tha could hang tha faw Him,
He had tuh hang tha by His-sef.

You got tuh join that Christian Army,
You got tuh join it by yo-sef;
No one heah to join it faw you,
You got tuh join it by yo'sef.

You got tuh live a life of service,
You got tuh live it by yo'sef;
No one heah to live it faw you,
You got tuh live it by yo'sef.

# WHEN I DIE

Who's gon—na make up muh dy—in' bed? Who's a—gon—na

make up muh dy——in' bed ——? Who's a gon——na

make up muh dy—in' bed ———————— when I ————

die —— when I ————— die? Je—sus gon—na

make up muh dy—in' bed —— Je—sus gon——na

make up muh dy ——— in' bed ———— Je—sus gon—na

make up muh dy —— in' bed ——— when I — die ——

# WHEN I DIE

Who's gonna make up muh dyin' bed?
Who's a gonna make up muh dyin' bed?
Who's a gonna make up muh dyin' bed,
When I die, when I die?
Jesus gonna make up muh dyin' bed,
Jesus gonna make up muh dyin' bed;
Jesus gonna make up muh dyin' bed,
      When I die.

Who's goin' down in duh grave wid me?
Who's a goin' down in duh grave wid me?
Who's a goin' down in duh grave wid me,
When I die, when I die?
Jesus goin' down in duh grave wid me,
Jesus goin' down in duh grave wid me;
Jesus goin' down in duh grave wid me,
      When I die.

Who's gonna sing that las' song?
Who's a gonna sing that las' song?
Who's a gonna sing that las' song,
When I die, when I die?
Jesus gonna sing that las' song,
Jesus gonna sing that las' song;
Jesus gonna sing that las' song,
      When I die.

Who's gonna pray that las' prayer?
Who's a gonna pray that las' prayer?
Who's a gonna pray that las' prayer,
When I die, when I die?
Jesus gonna pray that las' prayer,
Jesus gonna pray that las' prayer;
Jesus gonna pray that las' prayer,
      When I die.

Who's gonna take muh soul tuh Heaben?
Who's a gonna take muh soul tuh Heaben?
Who's a gonna take muh soul tuh Heaben,
When I die, when I die?
Jesus gonna take muh soul tuh Heaben,
Jesus gonna take muh soul tuh Heaben;
Jesus gonna take muh soul tuh Heaben,
      When I die.

I'm gonna treat ev'ry body right,
I'm a gonna treat ev'ry body right;
I'm a gonna treat ev'ry body right,
Tel I die, tel I die.
I'm gonna treat ev'ry body right,
I'm a gonna treat ev'ry body right;
I'm a gonna treat ev'ry body right,
      Tel I die.

I'm gonna stay on the battlefield,
I'm a gonna stay on the battlefield;
I'm a gonna stay on the battlefield,
Tel I die, tel I die.
I'm gonna stay on the battlefield,
I'm a gonna stay on the battlefield;
I'm a gonna stay on the battlefield,
      Tel I die.

I'm gonna take a soldier's fare,
I'm a gonna take a soldier's fare;
I'm a gonna take a soldier's fare,
Tel I die, tel I die.
I'm gonna take a soldier's fare,
I'm a gonna take a soldier's fare;
I'm a gonna take a soldier's fare,
      Tel I die.

# TELL 'EM I'M GONE

When you miss me from round ———— the fiah-

———— side ———— Tell 'em I'm gone = n tell 'em I'm

gone When you miss me from round ———— the fiah

—side— Tell 'em I'm gone = n Tell 'em I'm

gone—Tell 'em Death has sev — vud me ————

-uh Way o—vah in the Rock of A————ges

———— (or)  Tell 'em I'm gone — Tell 'em I'm gone ————
Clef fuh me ———— Clef fuh me ————

# TELL 'EM I'M GONE

When you miss me from round the fiahside,
   Tell 'em I'm gone; tell 'em I'm gone.
When you miss me from round the fiahside,
   Tell 'em I'm gone. Tell 'em I'm gone.
Tell 'em Death has sevvud me.
   Way ovah in the Rock of Ages,
   Clef fuh me—Clef fuh me.

When you miss me from singin' an' prayin',
   Tell 'em I'm gone; tell 'em I'm gone.
When you miss me from singin' an' prayin',
   Tell 'em I'm gone. Tell 'em I'm gone.
Tell 'em Death has sevvud me.
   Way ovah in the Rock of Ages,
   Clef fuh me—Clef fuh me.

When you miss me from the Sackament table,
   Tell 'em I'm gone; tell 'em I'm gone.
When you miss me from the Sackament table,
   Tell 'em I'm gone. Tell 'em I'm gone.
Tell 'em Death has sevvud me.
   Way ovah in the Rock of Ages,
   Clef fuh me—Clef fuh me.

When you miss me from weepin' an' moanin',
   Tell 'em I'm gone; tell 'em I'm gone.
When you miss me from weepin' an' moanin',
   Tell 'em I'm gone. Tell 'em I'm gone.
Tell 'em Death has sevvud me.
   Way ovah in the Rock of Ages,
   Clef fuh me—Clef fuh me.

When you miss me from the Amen corner,
   Tell 'em I'm gone; tell 'em I'm gone.
When you miss me from the Amen corner,
   Tell 'em I'm gone. Tell 'em I'm gone.
Tell 'em Death has sevvud me.
   Way ovah in the Rock of Ages,
   Clef fuh me—Clef fuh me.

When you miss me from the big baptizin',
   Tell 'em I'm gone; tell 'em I'm gone.
When you miss me from the big baptizin',
   Tell 'em I'm gone. Tell 'em I'm gone.
Tell 'em Death has sevvud me.
   Way ovah in the Rock of Ages,
   Clef fuh me—Clef fuh me.

When you miss me from the big revival,
   Tell 'em I'm gone; tell 'em I'm gone.
When you miss me from the big revival,
   Tell 'em I'm gone. Tell 'em I'm gone.
Tell 'em Death has sevvud me.
   Way ovah in the Rock of Ages,
   Clef fuh me—Clef fuh me.

# SOON ONE MAWNIN' DEATH COME CREEPIN'
## IN YO' ROOM

Soon one maw—nin', Death come creep-in' in yo' room

Soon one maw —— nin' Death come creep-in' in yo' Room HaHe-lu-jah Well

soon one maw—nin' Death come creep-in' in yo' room. Oh my

Lawd, Oh my Lawd what shall I —— do.

## SOON ONE MAWNIN' DEATH COME CREEPIN' IN YO' ROOM

Soon one mawnin' Death come creepin' in yo' room,
Soon one mawnin' Death come creepin' in yo' room,
      Hallelujah! Well
Soon one mawnin' Death come creepin' in yo' room.
Oh my Lawd, Oh my Lawd, what shall I do?

Soon one mawnin' Death come knockin' at yo' do',
Soon one mawnin' Death come knockin' at yo' do',
      Hallelujah! Well
Soon one mawnin' Death come knockin' at yo' do'.
Oh my Lawd, Oh my Lawd, what shall I do?

Hush! Hush! There's some one callin' mah name,
Hush! Hush! There's some one callin' mah name,
      Hallelujah! Well
Hush! Hush! There's some one callin' mah name.
Oh my Lawd, Oh my Lawd, what shall I do?

I'm so glad I belong to the church of God,
I'm so glad I belong to the church of God,
      Hallelujah! Well
I'm so glad I belong to the church of God.
Oh my Lawd, Oh my Lawd, what shall I do?

I'm so glad I can pray like the Savior prayed,
I'm so glad I can pray like the Savior prayed,
      Hallelujah! Well
I'm so glad I can pray like the Savior prayed.
Oh my Lawd, Oh my Lawd, what shall I do?

I'm so glad that Jesus will call mah name,
I'm so glad that Jesus will call mah name,
      Hallelujah! Well
I'm so glad that Jesus will call mah name.
Oh my Lawd, Oh my Lawd, what shall I do?

I'm so glad that trouble doan last always,
I'm so glad that trouble doan last always,
      Hallelujah! Well
I'm so glad that trouble doan last always.
Oh my Lawd, Oh my Lawd, what shall I do?

# LITTLE BLACK TRAIN IS A COMIN'

## LITTLE BLACK TRAIN IS A COMIN'

God tole Hezykiyah
In a message from on high:
Go set yo' house in ordah,
For thou shalt sholy die.
He turned to the wall an' a weepin',
Oh! See the King in tears;
He got his bus'ness fixed all right,
God spared him fifteen years.

CHORUS
*Little black train is a comin',*
*Get all yo' bus'ness right;*
*Go set yo' house in ordah,*
*For the train may be here tonight.*

Go tell that ball room lady,
All filled with worldly pride,
That little black train is-a comin',
Prepare to take a ride.
That little black train and engine
An' a little baggage car,
With idle thoughts and wicked deeds,
Must stop at the judgment bar.

There was a po' young man in darkness,
Cared not for the gospel light,
Suddenly a whistle blew
From a little black train in sight.
"Oh, death will you not spare me?
I'm just in my wicked plight.
Have mercy Lord, do hear me,
Pray come an' set me right."
But death had fixed his shackles
About his soul so tight,
Just befo' he got his bus'ness fixed,
The train rolled in that night.

Songs of Heaven and Resurrection

# OH MARY - OH MARTHY

Oh — Ma-ry Oh Mar-thy go tell my dis-ci-ples Gwine—a

meet Him in Gal-la—lee—Gwine-a meet Him in Gal-la-lee, Yes bless de Lawd

meet Him in Gal—la—lee — Gwine-a meet Him in Gal—la — lee.

*LEADER*

Oh yon-dah come duh Char-et, duh hos-ses dressed in white— duh

fo' wheels-a run—nin' by duh Grace ob God an' duh

hin' wheels-a run—nin' by love ——— an' duh

hin' wheels — a —— run—nin' by love.

## OH MARY—OH MARTHY

*Oh! Mary, Oh! Marthy, go tell my disciples,*
*Gwine-a meet Him in Gallalee,*
*Gwine-a meet Him in Gallalee.*
*Yes, bless de Lawd, meet Him in Gallalee.*
*Gwine-a meet Him in Gallalee.*

Oh! yondah come duh charet,
Duh hosses dressed in white,
Duh fo' wheels a runnin' by duh grace ob God,
An' duh hin' wheels a runnin' by love;
An' duh hin' wheels a runnin' by love.

Oh! yondah come ole Satan
Wid a black book under his arm;
A hollerin' give me jestice,
Mo'n hafen dem people am mine,
Mo'n hafen dem people am mine.
Yes, bless de Lawd, hafen dem people am mine;
Mo'n hafen dem people am mine.

Oh! yondah come Brudder Peter,
An' how do you know it's him?
Wid a crown upon his fo'head
An' de keys of Bethlyham,
An' de keys of Bethlyham.
Yes, bless de Lawd, keys of Bethlyham;
An' de keys of Bethlyham.

Oh! yondah come Sista Mary,
An' how do you know it's huhr?
A shoutin' Hallelujah
An' praises to duh Lamb,
An' praises to duh Lamb.
Yes, bless de Lawd, praises to duh **Lamb**;
An' praises to duh Lamb.

# WHEN I'M GONE

# WHEN I'M GONE

*It'll be Lawd, Lawd, Lawd,*
*    When I'm gone;*
*It'll be Lawd, Lawd, Lawd,*
*    When I'm gone.*
*It'll be Lawd, Lawd, Lawd,*
*It'll be Lawd, Lawd, Lawd,*
*It'll be Lawd, Lawd, Lawd,*
*    When I'm gone.*

I'm gonna fly from manshun to manshun,
    When I'm gone;
I'm gonna fly from manshun to manshun,
    When I'm gone.
I'm gonna fly from manshun to manshun,
Gonna fly from manshun to manshun,
Gonna fly from manshun to manshun,
    When I'm gone.

I'll be done wid 'bukes an' 'buses,*
    When I'm gone;
I'll be done wid 'bukes an' 'buses,
    When I'm gone.
I'll be done wid 'bukes an' 'buses,
Be done wid 'bukes an' 'buses,
Be done wid 'bukes an' 'buses,
    When I'm gone.

I'll be done wid troubles an' trials,
    When I'm gone;
I'll be done wid troubles an' trials,
    When I'm gone.
I'll be done wid troubles an' trials,
Be done wid troubles an' trials,
Be done wid troubles an' trials,
    When I'm gone.

I'm gonna walk an' talk wid Jesus,
    When I'm gone;
I'm gonna walk an' talk wid Jesus,
    When I'm gone.
I'm gonna walk an' talk wid Jesus,
Gonna walk an' talk wid Jesus,
Gonna walk an' talk wid Jesus,
    When I'm gone.

I'm gonna set down at de welcome table,
    When I'm gone;
I'm gonna set down at de welcome table,
    When I'm gone.
I'm gonna set down at de welcome table,
Gonna set down at de welcome table,
Gonna set down at de welcome table,
    When I'm gone.

I'm gonna drink an' nevuh get thirsty,
    When I'm gone;
I'm gonna drink an' nevuh get thirsty,
    When I'm gone.
I'm gonna drink an' nevuh get thirsty,
Gonna drink an' nevuh get thirsty,
Gonna drink an' nevuh get thirsty,
    When I'm gone.

* Rebukes and abuses.

# 'WAY IN THE KINGDOM

# 'WAY IN THE KINGDOM

*There's plenty-uh room, plenty-uh room,*
*'Way in the Kingdom;*
*There's plenty-uh good room where muh Jesus is,*
*'Way in the Kingdom.*

Mary had a link an' chain,
    'Way in the Kingdom;
An' every link was-a Jesus name,
    'Way in the Kingdom.
There's plenty-uh room, plenty-uh room,
    'Way in the Kingdom;
There's plenty-uh good room where muh Jesus is,
    'Way in the Kingdom.

He gimme the word an' he tole me to go,
    'Way in the Kingdom;
He gimme the trumpet an' he tole me to blow,
    'Way in the Kingdom.
There's plenty-uh room, plenty-uh room,
    'Way in the Kingdom;
There's plenty-uh good room where muh Jesus is,
    'Way in the Kingdom.

Jesus done jes' what he said,
    'Way in the Kingdom;
Healed the sick an'-a raised the dead,
    'Way in the Kingdom.
There's plenty-uh room, plenty-uh room,
    'Way in the Kingdom;
There's plenty-uh good room where muh Jesus is,
    'Way in the Kingdom.

One day 'bout twelve o'clock,
    'Way in the Kingdom;
He place-uh muh feet on the solid rock,
    'Way in the Kingdom.
There's plenty-uh room, plenty-uh room,
    'Way in the Kingdom;
There's plenty-uh good room where muh Jesus is,
    'Way in the Kingdom.

I nevah shall forget the day,
    'Way in the Kingdom;
That Jesus washed-uh my sins away,
    'Way in the Kingdom.
There's plenty-uh room, plenty-uh room,
    'Way in the Kingdom;
There's plenty-uh good room where muh Jesus is,
    'Way in the Kingdom.

# SOME O' THESE DAYS

MODERATE

I'm —— gon-na tell God how you treat ——

me —— I'm —— gon-na tell God how you

treat me some o' these days Hal-le-lu-jah, I'm— gon na

tell God how you treat —— me I'm gon-na

(SLOWER)

tell God how- you treat me some o' these days——

# SOME O' THESE DAYS

I'm gonna tell God how you treat me,
I'm gonna tell God how you treat me,
  Some o' these days.  Hallelujah!
I'm gonna tell God how you treat me,
I'm gonna tell God how you treat me,
  Some o' these days.

I'm gonna cross thuh river of Jurdun,
I'm gonna cross thuh river of Jurdun,
  Some o' these days.  Hallelujah!
I'm gonna cross thuh river of Jurdun,
I'm gonna cross thuh river of Jurdun,
  Some o' these days.

I'm gonna drink uv thuh healin' waters,
I'm gonna drink uv thuh healin' waters,
  Some o' these days.  Hallelujah!
I'm gonna drink uv thuh healin' waters,
I'm gonna drink uv thuh healin' waters,
  Some o' these days.

I'm gonna drink an' nevuh get thirsty,
I'm gonna drink an' nevuh get thirsty,
  Some o' these days.  Hallelujah!
I'm gonna drink an' nevuh get thirsty,
I'm gonna drink an' nevuh get thirsty,
  Some o' these days.

I'm gonna eat off thuh welcome table,
I'm gonna eat off thuh welcome table,
  Some o' these days.  Hallelujah!
I'm gonna eat off thuh welcome table,
I'm gonna eat off thuh welcome table,
  Some o' these days.

I'm gonna walk an' talk wid Jesus,
I'm gonna walk an' talk wid Jesus,
  Some o' these days.  Hallelujah!
I'm gonna walk an' talk wid Jesus,
I'm gonna walk an' talk wid Jesus,
  Some o' these days.

I'm gonna ride in thuh charet wid Jesus,
I'm gonna ride in thuh charet wid Jesus,
  Some o' these days.  Hallelujah!
I'm gonna ride in thuh charet wid Jesus,
I'm gonna ride in thuh charet wid Jesus,
  Some o' these days.

I'm gonna shout an' not be weary,
I'm gonna shout an' not be weary,
  Some o' these days.  Hallelujah!
I'm gonna shout an' not be weary,
I'm gonna shout an' not be weary,
  Some o' these days.

You're gonna wish that you'd-a been ready,
You're gonna wish that you'd-a been ready,
  Some o' these days.  Hallelujah!
You're gonna wish that you'd-a been ready,
You're gonna wish that you'd-a been ready,
  Some o' these days.

God's gonna set yo' sins befo' you,
God's gonna set yo' sins befo' you,
  Some o' these days.  Hallelujah!
God's gonna set yo' sins befo' you,
God's gonna set yo' sins befo' you,
  Some o' these days.

God's gonna bring this world to judgment,
God's gonna bring this world to judgment,
  Some o' these days.  Hallelujah!
God's gonna bring this world to judgment,
God's gonna bring this world to judgment,
  Some o' these days.

# HEAVEN IS A BEAUTIFUL PLACE

Hea—ven is a beau·ti—ful place I know ———— It

aint no ly—yuhs in Hea-ven I know ——— If you

wawn-ta get to Hea-ven on time ——————— you

she got to plumb the line ——— Hea-ven is a

beau ti ful place I know ——————

# HEAVEN IS A BEAUTIFUL PLACE

Heaven is a beautiful place,
    I know;
It ain't no lyuhs in Heaven,
    I know.
If you wawn-ta get to Heaven on time,
You sho got to plumb the line.
Heaven is a beautiful place,
    I know.

Heaven is a beautiful place,
    I know;
It ain't no gamblers in Heaven,
    I know.
If you wawn-ta get to Heaven on time,
You sho got to plumb the line.
Heaven is a beautiful place,
    I know.

Heaven is a beautiful place,
    I know;
It ain't no drunkards in Heaven,
    I know.
If you wawn-ta get to Heaven on time,
You sho got to plumb the line.
Heaven is a beautiful place,
    I know.

Heaven is a beautiful place,
    I know;
It ain't no sinners in Heaven,
    I know.
If you wawn-ta get to Heaven on time,
You sho got to plumb the line.
Heaven is a beautiful place,
    I know.

Heaven is a beautiful place,
    I know;
It ain't no troubles in Heaven,
    I know.
If you wawn-ta get to Heaven on time,
You sho got to plumb the line.
Heaven is a beautiful place,
    I know.

# I'LL BE SLEEPIN' IN MAH GRAVE

When He calls me I will an—swer I'll be some—where sleep—in' in mah grave. When He calls me I will an—swer I'll be some—where—sleep—in' in mah grave. I'll be sleep—in' in mah grave I'll be sleep-in' in mah grave I'll be some—where sleep—in' in mah grave I'll be sleep—in' in mah grave I'll be sleep—in' in mah grave I'll be some—where—sleep—in' in mah grave.

# I'LL BE SLEEPIN' IN MAH GRAVE

When He calls me I will answer,
    I'll be somewhere sleepin' in mah grave;
When He calls me I will answer,
    I'll be somewhere sleepin' in mah grave.

CHORUS.
*I'll be sleepin' in mah grave,*
*I'll be sleepin' in mah grave,*
*I'll be somewhere sleepin' in mah grave.*
*I'll be sleepin' in mah grave,*
*I'll be sleepin' in mah grave,*
*I'll be somewhere sleepin' in mah grave.*

When the Master calls us to Him,
    I'll be somewhere sleepin' in mah grave;
When the Master calls us to Him,
    I'll be somewhere sleepin' in mah grave.

In that great day when He calls me,
    I'll be somewhere sleepin' in mah grave;
In that great day when He calls me,
    I'll be somewhere sleepin' in mah grave.

NOTE—This song, as well as many others of this type, is always accompanied by hand clapping and foot motions in contrasting note groups. It is characteristic of so many songs now used in the Negro churches that it is accorded a place in this collection. It is of no great value except that it shows the influence of the cheap music used in the white man's church.

Bible Stories in Song

# MY GOD HE IS A MAN OF WAR

# MY GOD IS A MAN OF WAR

*My God He is a Man—a Man of war,*
*My God He is a Man—a Man of war,*
*My God He is a Man—a Man of war,*
*An' de Lawd God is His name.*

Ho tole Noah to build an ark,
    By His Holy plan;
He tole Moses to lead the chillun,
    From Egypt to the Promised Lan'.
My God He is a Man—a Man of war,
My God He is a Man—a Man of war,
My God He is a Man—a Man of war,
    An' de Lawd God is His name.

Long befo' the flyin' clouds,
    Befo' the heavens above,
Befo' creation evuh was made,
    He had redeemin' love.
My God He is a Man—a Man of war,
My God He is a Man—a Man of war,
My God He is a Man—a Man of war,
    An' de Lawd God is His name.

He made the sun an' moon an' stahrs,
    To rule both day an' night;
He placed them in the firmament,
    An' told them to give light.
My God He is a Man—a Man of war,
My God He is a Man—a Man of war,
My God He is a Man—a Man of war,
    An' de Lawd God is His name.

He made the birds of the air,
    An' made the earth aroun';
He made the beasts of the field,
    An' made the serpents on the groun'.
My God He is a Man—a Man of war,
My God He is a Man—a Man of war,
My God He is a Man—a Man of war,
    An' de Lawd God is His name.

# I MEAN TO LIFT UP A STANDARD FOR MY KING

CHORUS (Animated)

I mean to lift up a stan—dard faw my King. All

o—vuh this world I mean to sing— I mean to sing.

(Chant-like)

When Dan-iel was called by wick-ed men— They

cast po' Dan—iel in de li — yun's den —

Dan-iel went down— feel–in no fear. Be

cause he knew— his God was near. I mean to

Fine.

D.S. al Fine.

# I MEAN TO LIFT UP A STANDARD FOR MY KING

*I mean to lift up a standard faw my King,*
*All ovuh this world I mean to sing.*

When Daniel was called by wicked men,
They cast po' Daniel in de liyun's den;
Daniel went down feelin' no fear,
Because he knew his God was near.
I mean to lift up a standard faw my King,
All ovuh this world I mean to sing.

When Daniel found out a writin' was signed,
He went to his room in his own set time;
He fell on his knees an' begin to pray,
An' in this sperit I heard him say:
I mean to lift up a standard faw my King,
All ovuh this world I mean to sing.

When the King had signed that wicked decree,
Daniel was found down on his knees;
"I'm goin' to pray three times a day,
An' look to Jesus to open the way."
I mean to lift up a standard faw my King,
All ovuh this world I mean to sing.

The King was in trouble all night long,
He felt that he treated po' Daniel wrong;
He went down early next mawnin' to see,
"King, the God I serve has delivud me."
I mean to lift up a standard faw my King,
All ovah this world I mean to sing.

# EZEKIEL'S WHEEL

# EZEKIEL'S WHEEL

*'Zekus' wheel—Oh, my soul!*
*E'Zekus' wheel—Oh, my soul!*
*Uh 'Zekus' wheel—Oh, my soul!*
*Le's take a ride awn-uh 'Zekus' wheel.*

There's 'ligion in the wheel,
   Oh, my soul!
There's 'ligion in the wheel,
   Oh, my soul!
'Ligion in the wheel,
   Oh, my soul!
Le's take a ride awn-uh 'Zekus' wheel.

There's moanin' in the wheel,
   Oh, my soul!
There's moanin' in the wheel,
   Oh, my soul!
Moanin' in the wheel,
   Oh, my soul!
Le's take a ride awn-uh 'Zekus' wheel.

There's prayin' in the wheel,
   Oh, my soul!
There's prayin' in the wheel,
   Oh, my soul!
Prayin' in the wheel,
   Oh, my soul!
Le's take a ride awn-uh 'Zekus' wheel.

There's shoutin' in the wheel,
   Oh, my soul!
There's shoutin' in the wheel,
   Oh, my soul!
Shoutin' in the wheel,
   Oh, my soul!
Le's take a ride awn-uh 'Zekus' wheel.

There's cryin' in the wheel,
   Oh, my soul!
There's cryin' in the wheel,
   Oh, my soul!
Cryin' in the wheel,
   Oh, my soul!
Le's take a ride awn-uh 'Zekus' wheel.

There's laughin' in the wheel,
   Oh, my soul!
There's laughin' in the wheel,
   Oh, my soul!
Laughin' in the wheel,
   Oh, my soul!
Le's take a ride awn-uh 'Zekus' wheel.

# MARY WEPT AN' MARTHY MOANED

# MARY WEPT AN' MARTHY MOANED

Mary wept an'-a Marthy moaned,
Mary wept an'-a Marthy moaned,
Mary wept an'-a Marthy moaned,
   Round a willuh tree.
   Round a willuh tree.

Who's-a been heah since I've been gone?
Who's-a been heah since I've been gone?
Who's-a been heah since I've been gone?
Good Lawd done come an' gone.
Good Lawd done come an' gone.

I don' wan-tuh live an' die in sin,
I don' wan-tuh live an' die in sin,
I don' wan-tuh live an' die in sin,
Good Lawd delivuh me.
Good Lawd delivuh me.

NOTE—This song is sometimes sung with the lower line, "King Jesus bowed His head an' groaned," as indicated in the music.

# I BELIEVE I'LL GO BACK HOME

# I BELIEVE I'LL GO BACK HOME

*I believe I'll go back home,*
*I believe I'll go back home,*
*I believe I'll go back home,*
*An' acknowledge I done wrong.*

When I was in my Father's house,
I was well supplied;
I made a mistake in doin' well,
An' now I'm dissatisfied.

When I was in my Father's house,
I had peace all the time;
But when I left home an' went astray,
I had to feed the swine.

When the Prodigal Son first left home,
He was feelin' happy an' gay;
But he soon found out a riotous life
Was more than he could pay.

When I was in my Father's house,
I had bread enough to spare;
But now I am naked an' hungry, too,
An' I am ashamed to go back there.

When I left home I was in royal robes,
An' sumptuously fed;
But I soon got ragged an' hungry, too,
An' come back home so sad.

When I get home I'll confess my sins,
And Father's love embrace;
I'm no more worthy to be called thy son,
I'll seek a servant's place.

When his Father saw him comin',
He met him with a smile;
He threw his arms around him . . .
"Here comes my lovin' child!"

He spake unto his servants—
"Go kill the fatted calf;
An' call my friends an' neighbors,
My son has come at last."

His oldest son got jealous,
And he began to say:
"You did more for my brother,
Who left an' went away."

He spake unto his eldest son—
It was with an humble mind—
"Son, you have always been with me,
An' all I have is thine."

They met together rejoicing,
I imagine it was fine;
The old man he got happy,
An' he was satisfied in mind.

NOTE—This is an excellent version of the many Negro songs about the "Prodigal Son."

# JOHN DONE SAW DAT NUMBUH

John done saw dat num — buh — 'Way in de mid-dle of de

air; Don't chu wawn-ta jine dat num-buh 'Way in de mid-dle of de

air; On de right I saw a sight 'Way — in de mid dle of de

air; A band of An—gels dressed in white 'Way —— in de mid-dle of de air.

## JOHN DONE SAW DAT NUMBUH

*John done saw dat numbuh,*
  *'Way in de middle of de air;*
*Don't-chu wanta jine dat numbuh,*
  *'Way in de middle of de air?*

On de right I saw a sight,
  'Way in de middle of de air;
A band of Angels dressed in white,
  'Way in de middle of de air.

Havin' great tribulations,
  'Way in de middle of de air;
Havin' their harps in their han's,
  'Way in de middle of de air.

Singin' a new song before the throne,
  'Way in de middle of de air;
That Angels in Heabum could not sing,
  'Way in de middle of de air.

John done saw dat numbuh,
  'Way in de middle of de air;
Comin' up from hard triyuls,
  'Way in de middle of de air.

On de left I saw no rest,
  'Way in de middle of de air.
I'm gonna talk 'bout God myse'f,
  'Way in de middle of de air.

# Songs of Exhortation

# IT MAY BE DE LAS' TIME

M: 44 (♩)

CHORUS

Oh it may be Oh it may be Oh — it

— m - may be, it may be duh las' time - uh I dun — no

(deliberately)

LEADER                                    RESPONSE

Come aw — n sin — nuh Come awn a — cross ———— It

may be duh las' time — uh — I dun — no

LEADER                                    RESPONSE

Come aw — n sin — nuh doan' step on duh Cross ———— It

may be duh las' time, I dun — no.

# IT MAY BE DE LAS' TIME

*Oh, it may be,*
*Oh, it may be,*
*Oh, it may be,*
*It may be duh las' time-uh*
*I dunno.*

Come awn sinnuh, come awn across,
It may be duh las' time-uh.
    I dunno.
Come awn sinnuh, doan' step on duh Cross,
It may be duh las' time.
    I dunno.

Look out sinnuh how you step on duh Cross,
It may be duh las' time-uh.
    I dunno.
Yo' foot might slip an' yo' soul get lost,
It may be duh las' time.
    I dunno.

Sinnuh man you bettuh pray,
It may be duh las' time-uh.
    I dunno.
It woan' be long 'tel Jedgment Day,
It may be duh las' time.
    I dunno.

The Bible warns you day by day,
It may be duh las' time-uh.
    I dunno.
That you got tuh change yo' wicked way,
It may be duh las' time.
    I dunno.

## OH SINNER

Oh sin—nuh yo' bed's too short ———— Oh ———— sin—nuh yo' bed's too short ———— Oh— sin—nuh yo' bed's too short ———— Um — — — — — — My Lawd .

## OH SINNER

Oh, sinnuh, yo' bed's too short,
Oh, sinnuh, yo' bed's too short,
Oh, sinnuh, yo' bed's too short,
Um . . . . . My Lawd.

Oh, sinnuh, you better pray,
Oh, sinnuh, you better pray,
Oh, sinnuh, you better pray,
Um . . . . . My Lawd.

Oh, sinnuh, yo' time ain't long,
Oh, sinnuh, yo' time ain't long,
Oh, sinnuh, yo' time ain't long,
Um . . . . . My Lawd.

Ev'ry body's got tuh die sometime,
Ev'ry body's got tuh die sometime,
Ev'ry body's got tuh die sometime,
Um . . . . . My Lawd.

I'm goin' home awn duh mawnin' train,
I'm goin' home awn duh mawnin' train,
I'm goin' home awn duh mawnin' train,
Um . . . . . My Lawd.

*Kindness of Miss Alice Camp,*
*Gadsden, Alabama.*

# WALK ABOUT ELDERS

# WALK ABOUT ELDERS

*Walk about Elders, Jesus a listenin';*
*Walk about Elders, Jesus died.*

Paul an' Silus bound in jail,
Paul an' Silus a-bound in jail;
Paul an' Silus a-bound in jail,
Nothin' but the blood of Jesus can pay their bail.
    Walk about Elders, Jesus a listenin';
    Walk about Elders, Jesus died.

Good ole Daniel in de Lion's Den,
Good ole Daniel in de Lion's Den;
Good ole Daniel in de Lion's Den,
None but de lowly Jesus was his frien'.
    Walk about Elders, Jesus a listenin';
    Walk about Elders, Jesus died.

While de rich man lived he lived so well,
While de rich man lived he lived so well;
While de rich man lived he lived so well,
When he died he made his home in Hell.
    Walk about Elders, Jesus a listenin';
    Walk about Elders, Jesus died.

When you see me standin' round,
When you see me standin' round;
When you see me standin' round,
You jes' can know that I am Heaven bound.
    Walk about Elders, Jesus a listenin';
    Walk about Elders, Jesus died.

# GIT YO' TICKET

Git yo' tick—et — — — — — Git yo' tick—et — — — — Git yo'

tick—et  Good  Lawd—Git  yo'  tick—et — — —  Oh

When,  when,  when,  Oh — — — —  when ?

# GIT YO' TICKET

Git yo' ticket,
Git yo' ticket,
Git yo' ticket, Good Lawd.
Git yo' ticket,
Oh! When, when, when,
Oh! When?

Train's a-comin',
Train's a-comin',
Train's a-comin', Good Lawd.
Train's a-comin',
Oh! When, when, when,
Oh! When?

Bound for Glory,
Bound for Glory,
Bound for Glory, Good Lawd.
Bound for Glory,
Oh! When, when, when,
Oh! When?

I can tell it,
I can tell it,
I can tell it, Good Lawd.
I can tell it,
Oh! When, when, when,
Oh! When?

I can read it,
I can read it,
I can read it, Good Lawd.
I can read it,
Oh! When, when, when,
Oh! When?

I can live it,
I can live it,
I can live it, Good Lawd.
I can live it,
Oh! When, when, when,
Oh! When?

I can sing it,
I can sing it,
I can sing it, Good Lawd.
I can sing it,
Oh! When, when, when,
Oh! When?

Judgmunt's comin',
Judgmunt's comin',
Judgmunt's comin', Good Lawd.
Judgmunt's comin',
Oh! When, when, when,
Oh! When?

# COME UNTO ME

# COME UNTO ME

*Can't you heah what my Lawd said,*
*Can't you heah what my Lawd said,*
*Can't You heah?*
*Can't you heah what my Lawd said,*
*Come unto me an' be saved.*

Oh, if you are a gambler,
Come unto me,
Come unto me,
Come unto me.
Oh, if you are gambler,
Come unto me.
Come unto me an' be saved.

Oh, if you are a liah,
Come unto me,
Come unto me,
Come unto me.
Oh, if you are a liah,
Come unto me.
Come unto me an' be saved.

Oh, if you are a murderuh,
Come unto me,
Come unto me,
Come unto me.
Oh, if you are a murderuh,
Come unto me.
Come unto me an' be saved.

Oh, if you are a sinnuh,
Come unto me,
Come unto me,
Come unto me,
Oh, if you are a sinnuh,
Come unto me.
Come unto me an' be saved.

# YO' SINS ARE GONNA FIND YOU OUT

You can run a long time with the cov-uh of the world pulled-a-
o-vah yo' face —— you can run a long time but yo'
sins uh — gon — na find you out ——
We have some peo ple in de church you have
oft — en heard it said —— You can-not live that
ho — ly life 'til you git on yo' dy — in' bed. —

# YO' SINS ARE GONNA FIND YOU OUT

*You can run a long time*
*With the covuh of the world pulled a'ovah yo' face;*
*You can run a long time,*
*But yo' sins uh gonna find you out.*

We have some people in de church,
You have often heard it said,
You cannot live that holy life
'Til you git on yo' dyin' bed.

We have some people in de church,
Who love to sing an 'pray;
They love to shout an' testify,
But take the Bible away.

Just let me tell you about a liar,
He will not do to trust;
He will tell a lie to make a fuss,
An' tell another to make it wuss.

I can see that sister shoutin',
She seems to be mighty glad;
But as soon as you preach the Bible true,
You are sure to make her mad.

We have some people in de church,
Believes in having two wives;
An' when you call him to council,
His temper will begin to rise.

We have some preachers in de church,
With a wife an' a sweetheart, too;
They seem to be living satisfied,
But God has a time for you.

Some preachers out a preachin',
Just for the preacher's name;
The gospel they are preachin',
It is a scandal an' a shame.

Preachers in the pulpit preachin',
Seem to talk mighty sweet;
But the reason they don't like holiness,
They want to court every sister they meet.

Some women love other women's husbands
They ought to be loving their own;
If you ain't got one you better get one,
To be ready when the judgment comes.

You say you been converted,
Be sure you have not lied;
They tell me in my Father's house,
They are holy an' sanctified.

# TIME IS DRAWIN' NIGH

See the signs of the Judg — munt, Yes — see the

signs of the Judg — munt e-Yes —— see the

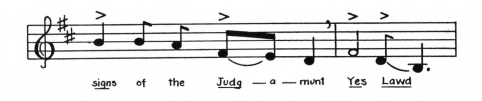

signs of the Judg — a — munt Yes Lawd

Time is draw —— in' nigh ——————.

# TIME IS DRAWIN' NIGH

See the signs of the Judgmunt, yes,
See the signs of the Judgmunt, yes,
See the signs of the Judgamunt, yes, Lawd,
Time is drawin' nigh.

God talkin' in the lightenin', yes,
An' He's talkin' in the thunder, yes,
An' the world's all a-wonder, yes, Lawd,
Time is drawin' nigh.

See the sign of the fig tree, yes,
My Jesus said it would be, yes,
The sign of the Judgmunt, yes, Lawd,
Time is drawin' nigh.

Loose horse in the valley, yes,
Don't you hear him laughin', yes,
He's laughin' like Judgamunt, yes, Lawd,
Time is drawin' nigh.

God told Moses, yes,
Sanctify the people, yes,
An' take to the mountains, yes, Lawd,
Time is drawin' nigh.

In the city of Jerusalem, yes,
On the day of Pentecost, yes.
The people received the Holy Ghost, Lawd,
Time is drawin' nigh.

Who is that yonduh, yes,
Comin' from Eden, yes,
Dyed garments from Bozah, yes, Lawd,
Time is drawin' nigh.

It looks like Jesus, yes,
Glorious in His appearance, yes,
Treadin' the wine press, yes, Lawd,
Time is drawin' nigh.

Thy Kingdom come, yes,
Thy will be done, yes,
They'll speak in other tongues, yes, Lawd,
Time is drawin' nigh.

They will hate one another, yes,
My Jesus said it would be, yes,
They'll take you in council, yes, Lawd,
Time is drawin' nigh.

Have you been converted, yes,
Sanctified an' holy, yes,
Baptized with the Holy Ghost, yes, Lawd,
Time is drawin' nigh.

I have my ticket, yes,
It takes a holy ticket, yes,
Signed all the way to glory, yes, Lawd,
Time is drawin' nigh.

Come on children, yes,
Let's go to glory, yes,
An' don't get tired, yes, Lawd,
Time is drawin' nigh.

Songs of Service and Personal Experience

# I'M AN EVERYDAY WITNESS

## I'M AN EVERYDAY WITNESS

*I'm a witness faw mah Lawd,*
*I'm a witness faw mah Lawd,*
*I'm a witness faw mah Lawd,*
*I'm a everday witness faw mah Lawd.*

I'm a Mondy witness faw mah Lawd,
I'm a Mondy witness faw mah Lawd,
I'm a Mondy witness faw mah Lawd,
I'm a everday witness faw mah Lawd.

I'm a Tuesdy witness faw mah Lawd,
I'm a Tuesdy witness faw mah Lawd,
I'm a Tuesdy witness faw mah Lawd,
I'm a everday witness faw mah Lawd.

I'm a Wednesdy witness faw mah Lawd,
I'm a Wednesdy witness faw mah Lawd,
I'm a Wednesdy witness faw mah Lawd, .
I'm a everday witness faw mah Lawd.

I'm a Thursdy witness faw mah Lawd,
I'm a Thursdy witness faw mah Lawd,
I'm a Thursdy witness faw mah Lawd,
I'm a everday witness faw mah Lawd.

I'm a Fridy witness faw mah Lawd,
I'm a Fridy witness faw mah Lawd,
I'm a Fridy witness faw mah Lawd,
I'm a everday witness faw mah Lawd.

I'm a Saturdy witness faw mah Lawd,
I'm a Saturdy witness faw mah Lawd,
I'm a Saturdy witness faw mah Lawd,
I'm a everday witness faw mah Lawd.

I'm a Sundy witness faw mah Lawd,
I'm a Sundy witness faw mah Lawd,
I'm a Sundy witness faw mah Lawd,
I'm a everday witness faw mah Lawd.

# IN THE ARMY OF THE LORD

# IN THE ARMY OF THE LORD

m a soljuh in the Army of thuh Lawd,
  I'm a soljuh in this Army;
m a soljuh in the Army of thuh Lawd,
  I'm a soljuh in this Army.
ll live again in the Army of thuh Lawd,
  I'll live again in this Army;
ll live again in the Army of thuh Lawd,
  I'll live again in this Army.

f a man dies in the Army of thuh Lawd,
  Ef a man dies in this Army;
f a man dies in the Army of thuh Lawd,
  Ef a man dies in this Army.
Ie'll live again in the Army of thuh Lawd,
  He'll live again in this Army;
Ie'll live again in the Army of thuh Lawd,
  He'll live again in this Army.

ve had a hahd time in the Army of thuh Lawd,
  Had a hahd time in this Army;
ve had a hahd time in the Army of thuh Lawd,
  Had a hahd time in this Army.
m fightin' faw mah rights in the Army
    of thuh Lawd,
  I'm fightin' faw mah rights in this Army;
m fightin' faw mah rights in the Army
    of thuh Lawd,
  I'm fightin' faw mah rights in this Army.

I've come a long way in the Army of thuh Lawd,
  Come along way in this Army;
I've come a long way in the Army of thuh Lawd,
  Come a long way in this Army.
Some day I'll rest in the Army of thuh Lawd,
  Some day I'll rest in this Army;
Some day I'll rest in the Army of thuh Lawd,
  Some day I'll rest in this Army.

My soul died in the Army of thuh Lawd,
  My soul died in this Army;
My soul died in the Army of thuh Lawd,
  My soul died in this Army.
It'll live again in the Army of thuh Lawd,
  It'll live again in this Army;
It'll live again in the Army of thuh Lawd,
  It'll live again in this Army.

Hosyannah, in the Army of thuh Lawd,
  Hosyannah, in this Army;
Hosyannah, in the Army of thuh Lawd,
  Hosyannah, in this Army.
We'll live again in the Army of thuh Lawd,
  We'll live again in this Army;
We'll live again in the Army of thuh Lawd,
  We'll live again in this Army.

My mother died in the Army of thuh Lawd,
  My mother died in this Army;
My mother died in the Army of thuh Lawd,
  My mother died in this Army.
She'll live again in the Army of thuh Lawd,
  She'll live again in this Army;
She'll live again in the Army of thuh Lawd,
  She'll live again in this Army.

# I WANTA LIVE SO GOD CAN USE ME

# I WANTA LIVE SO GOD CAN USE ME

I wanta live so God can use me,
 Victorious, in this lan';
I wanta live so God can use me,
 Victorious, in this lan'.

I wanta walk so God can use me,
 Victorious, in this lan';
I wanta walk so God can use me,
 Victorious, in this lan'.

I wanta pray so God can use me,
 Victorious, in this lan';
I wanta pray so God can use me,
 Victorious, in this lan'.

I wanta sing so God can use me,
 Victorious, in this lan';
I wanta sing so God can use me,
 Victorious, in this lan'.

I wanta work so God can use me,
 Victorious, in this lan';
I wanta work so God can use me,
 Victorious, in this lan'.

I wanta preach so God can use me,
 Victorious, in this lan';
I wanta preach so God can use me,
 Victorious, in this lan'.

Treat my sisters so God can use me,
 Victorious, in this lan';
Treat my sisters so God can use me,
 Victorious, in this lan'.

Treat my brothers so God can use me,
 Victorious, in this lan';
Treat my brothers so God can use me,
 Victorious, in this lan'.

Treat my children so God can use me,
 Victorious, in this lan';
Treat my children so God can use me,
 Victorious, in this lan'.

Treat my neighbors so God can use me,
 Victorious, in this lan';
Treat my neighbors so God can use me,
 Victorious, in this lan'.

# I GOT MAH SWOAD IN MAH HAN'

## I GOT MAH SWOAD IN MAH HAN'

*I got mah swoad in mah han',*
    *In mah han', Lawd;*
*I got mah swoad in mah han',*
    *Help me sing it.*
*I got my swoad in mah han',*
    *In mah han', Lawd;*
*I got my swoad in mah han'.*

I'm a-prayin', Lawd,
I got mah swoad in mah han';
    I'm a-prayin', Lawd,
I got mah swoad in mah han'.
    I'm a-preachin', Lawd,
I got mah swoad in mah han'.
    I'm a-preachin', Lawd,
I got mah swoad in mah han'.
    I'm a-shoutin', Lawd,
I got mah swoad in mah han'.
    I'm a-shoutin', Lawd,
I got mah swoad in mah han'.

My sister's in one place
    An' I in another;
Jedgmun' Day's a-gonna
    Bring us all together.   Well,
I got mah swoad, *etc.*

My mother's in one place
    An' I in another;
Jedgmun' Day's a-gonna
    Bring us all together.   Well,
I got my swoad, *etc.*

My father's in one place
    An' I in another;
Jedgmun' Day's a-gonna
    Bring us all together.   Well,
I got my swoad, *etc.*

My friends are in one place
    An' I in another;
Jedgmun' Day's a-gonna
    Bring us all together.   Well,
I got my swoad, *etc.*

# HIDE – A – ME

When this world is world is all on fi —— yuh Hide - a

me ————— When this world is —— all on

fi — yuh Hide – a me ——— When this

world is —— all on fi – yuh ——— Let Thy

bos — om be — my pil —— luh —— Hide me

O'er the Rock of A —— ges — Safe in Thee — .

# HIDE-A-ME

When this world is all on fiyuh,
    Hide-a-me;
When this world is all on fiyuh,
    Hide-a-me.
When this world is all on fiyuh,
Let Thy bosom be my pilluh,
Hide me o'er the Rock of Ages,
    Safe in Thee.

When the stars in heaven are fallin',
    Hide-a-me;
When the stars in heaven are fallin',
    Hide-a-me.
When the stars in heaven are fallin',
Let Thy bosom be my pilluh,
Hide me o'er the Rock of Ages,
    Safe in Thee.

When the trumpet sounds fuh judgmunt,
    Hide-a-me;
When the trumpet sounds fuh judgmunt.
    Hide-a-me.
When the trumpet sounds fuh judgmunt,
Let Thy bosom be my pilluh,
Hide me o'er the Rock of Ages,
    Safe in Thee.

When mah name is called at judgmunt,
    Hide-a-me;
When mah name is called at judgmunt,
    Hide-a-me.
When mah name is called at judgmunt,
Let Thy bosom be my pilluh,
Hide me o'er the Rock of Ages,
    Safe in Thee.

# DO LORD REMEMBER ME

# DO LORD REMEMBER ME

*Do Lawd, do Lawd, do remembuh me,*
*Do Lawd, do Lawd, do remembuh me,*
*Do Lawd, do Lawd, do remembuh me,*
*Do Lawd, remembuh me.*

When I'm sick an' by myself,
Do remembuh me;
When I'm sick an' by myself,
Do remembuh me.
When I'm sick an' by myself,
Do remembuh me,
Do, Lawd, remembuh me.

When I'm crossin' Jurdon,
Do remembuh me;
When I'm crossin' Jurdon,
Do remembuh me.
When I'm crossin' Jurdon,
Do remembuh me,
Do, Lawd, remembuh me.

If I ain't got no frien's at all,
Do remembuh me;
If I ain't got no frien's at all,
Do remembuh me.
If I ain't got no frien's at all,
Do remembuh me,
Do, Lawd, remembuh me.

Paul an' Silus bound in jail,
Do remembuh me;
Paul an' Silus bound in jail,
Do remembuh me.
Paul an' Silus bound in jail,
Do remembuh me,
Do, Lawd, remembuh me.

One did sing while the other one prayed,
Do remembuh me;
One did sing while the other one prayed,
Do remembuh me.
One did sing while the other one prayed,
Do remembuh me,
Do Lawd, remembuh me.

When I'm bound in trouble,
Do remembuh me;
When I'm bound in trouble,
Do remembuh me.
When I'm bound in trouble,
Do remembuh me,
Do, Lawd, remembuh me.

When I'm goin' from do' to do',
Do remembuh me;
When I'm goin' from do' to do',
Do remembuh me.
When I'm goin' from do' to do',
Do remembuh me,
Do, Lawd, remembuh me.

# IN THIS FIELD

Lord-y wont you hep me —— Lord-y wont you

hep me —————— Lord — y wont you

hep me ————— in this — field ————— .

## IN THIS FIELD

Lordy, won't you he'p me?
Lordy, won't you he'p me?
Lordy, won't you he'p me?
   In this field.

Troubles is so hard,
Troubles is so hard,
Troubles is so hard,
   In this field.

There's mo' than me, Lawd,
There's mo' than me, Lawd,
There's mo' than me, Lawd,
   In this field.

There's mo' to do, Lawd,
There's mo' to do, Lawd,
There's mo' to do, Lawd,
   In this field.

There's mo' to be won,
There's mo' to be won,
There's mo' to be won,
   In this field.

# WRING MY HANDS AND CRY

Some—times I – uh — feel like ———— a

moan ——— in' dove ———— Some-Times I ——— feel like a

moan ——— in' dove ———— Some — times I ———

feel — like ———— a – um – moan'–in' dove ————

Wring my han's an' cry ——— cry ——— cry ———

wring my han's an' cry ——————— cry ———

## WRING MY HANDS AND CRY

Sometimes I feel like
  A moanin' dove.
Sometimes I feel like
  A moanin' dove.
Sometimes I feel like
  A moanin' dove—
Wring my han's an'
  Cry, cry, cry;
Wring my han's an'
  Cry, cry.

Sometimes I feel like
  A motherless chile.
Sometimes I feel like
  A motherless chile.
Sometimes I feel like
  A motherless chile—
Wring my han's an'
  Cry, cry, cry;
Wring my han's an'
  Cry, cry.

Sometimes I feel like
  I gotta no home.
Sometimes I feel like
  I gotta no home.
Sometimes I feel like
  I gotta no home—
Wring my han's an'
  Cry, cry, cry;
Wring my han's an'
  Cry, cry.

Sometimes I'm troubled
  All day long.
Sometimes I'm troubled
  All day long.
Sometmes I'm troubled
  All day long—
Wring my han's an'
  Cry, cry, cry;
Wring my han's an'
  Cry, cry.

Sometimes I'm prayin'
  All day long.
Sometimes I'm prayin'
  All day long.
Sometimes I'm prayin'
  All day long—
Wring my han's an'
  Cry, cry, cry;
Wring my han's an'
  Cry, cry.

Sometimes I feel like
  I gotta no frien's.
Sometimes I feel like
  I gotta no frien's.
Sometimes I feel like
  I gotta no frien's—
Wring my han's an'
  Cry, cry, cry;
Wring my han's an'
  Cry, cry.

Sometimes I feel like
  A eagle in de air.
Sometimes I feel like
  A eagle in de air.
Sometimes I feel like
  A eagle in de air—
Spread my wings an'
  Fly, fly, fly;
Spread my wings an'
  Fly, fly.

# WISH I WAS IN HEABUM SETTIN' DOWN

I wish I was in Hea—bum set—tin' down set—tin' down I
wish I was in Hea—bum set—tin' down ———
Wish I was in Hea—bum Oh yes Oh — yes, I
wish I was in Hea—bum set—tin' down ——— .

## ANOTHER VERSION

I wish I was in Hea—bum set—tin' down ———
Wish I was in Hea—bum set—tin' down ———
Oh Rā—phēēl Oh ——— Lawd ——— I
wish I was in Hea—bum set—tin' down ——— .

[ 74 ]

## WISH I WAS IN HEABUM SETTIN' DOWN

I wish I was in Heabum settin' down, settin' down,
    I wish I was in Heabum settin' down;
Wish I was in Heabum—Oh, yes!  Oh, yes!
    I wish I was in Heabum settin' down.

In Heabum I wouldn't have nothin' a-tall to do, 'tall to do,
    In Heabum I wouldn't have nothin' a-tall to do;
Jes' set down an' rest—Oh, yes!  Oh, yes!
    In Heabum I wouldn't have nothin' a-tall to do.

I'd walk about in Heabum an' tell the news, tell the news,
    I'd walk about in Heabum an' tell the news;
Walk about in Heabum—Oh, yes!  Oh, yes!
    I'd walk about in Heabum an' tell the news.

# I STOOD OUTSIDE THE GATE

# I STOOD OUTSIDE THE GATE

I stood outside thay gate;
They would not let me in—me in.
I prayed to my good Lawd,
To cleanse me from all sin—all sin.

Lord Jesus Christ, I seek to find,
Pray tell me whar He dwells—He dwells.
Oh, you go down in yonder fold
An' search among the sheep—the sheep.

There you will find Him, I am told
He's whar He loves to be—to be.
An' if I find Him how'll I know
Round any other man—other man?

He has Salvation awn His brow,
He has a wounded han'—wounded han'.
I thank you faw yo' advice—
I'll find Him ef I can—ef I can.

Note—This type of singing is used particularly at funerals and very solemn occasions. It is rarely heard now. It probably has its origin in the old type of hymn-singing, used in the early church, in which the hymn was "lined" by a leader. When given with the Negro's peculiar style of chanting and sliding to and from the main melody note, it is distinctly a thing apart.

The example given here is purely Negro both in tune and words, but frequently one hears a well-known hymn chanted. The entire congregation sings in unison with each line of the verse chanted by the leader.

# STEAL AWAY TO MAH FATHUH'S KINGDOM

## STEAL AWAY TO MAH FATHUH'S KINGDOM

Steal away—steal away,
Steal away to mah Fathuh's Kingdom.
    Steal away.
Down in the valley,
    Steal away.
Talkin' to my Jesus,
    Steal away.
No mo' trouble,
    Steal away.
My Lawd with me,
    Steal away.
Steal away—steal away,
Steal away to mah Fathuh's Kingdom.
    Steal away.

Steal away—steal away,
Steal away to mah Fathuh's Kingdom.
    Steal away.
Down in the valley,
    Steal away.
Shoutin', Hallelujah!
    Steal away.
Free from hard trials,
    Steal away.
Jesus walkin' with me,
    Steal away.
Steal away—steal away,
Steal away to mah Fathuh's Kingdom.
    Steal away.

# LAWD I WANT TWO WINGS

# LAWD I WANT TWO WINGS

*Lawd, I want two wings to veil my face,*
*Lawd, I want two wings to fly away;*
*Lawd, I want two wings to veil my face,*
*Lawd, I want two wings to fly away.*

Jesus on the mountain
Preachin' to the po',
Never heard such a sermon
In all my life befo'.

Did not come in the mawnin',
Neither in the heat of the day;
But He always come in the evenin',
An' washed my sins away.

When you are in trouble,
Journeyin' on yo' way;
Jes' put yo' trust in Jesus,
An' don't forget to pray.

Git up in the mawnin',
Git up out-a yo' bed;
You should not eat one mouthful
Until yo' prayers are said.

I went down in the valley,
Hands across my breast;
Thought I heard King Jesus say—
Come unto me an' rest.

Yonder comes my mother—
Wha' you been so long?
Well, I been down in the valley,
My soul's done anchored an' gone.

Yonder comes that Angel—
What might be yo' name?
My name is Great Jehovah,
Well, you must be bawn again.

# IF I HAVE MAH TICKIT LAWD

CHORUS

If I have mah tick—it Lawd can I ride—

If I have mah tick it Lawd can I ride—a

If I have mah tick—it Lawd can I ride

Ride a way to Heav-en in that mawn—in'———

(LEADER) RECITATIVE

This is what we Chirst-chuns ought to do: Be

cer—tain an' sure— that we are liv—in' true for

bye an' bye — with — out a doubt Je —

ho vah's gon-na or-dah his An—gels out They will

clean out the world an' 'leave no sin — now

tell — me hy —po — crite whah you been——— .

## IF I HAVE MAH TICKIT LAWD

*If I have mah tickit, Lawd, can I ride?*
*If I have mah tickit, Lawd, can I ride-a?*
*If I have mah tickit, Lawd, can I ride?*
*Ride away to Heaven in that mawnin'.*

This is what we Christchuns ought to do;
Be certain an' sure that we are livin' true.
For bye an' bye, without a doubt,
Jehovah's gonna ordah his Angels out.
They will clean out the world an' leave no sin,
Now tell me, hypocrite, whah you been?

I heard the sound of the Gospel train,
Don't you want to get on? Yes, that's my aim.
I'll stand at the station an' patiently wait
For the train that's comin', an' she's never late.
You must have you ticket stamped bright an' clear,
Train is comin', she's drawin' near.

Hope to be ready when the train do come,
My ticket all right an' my work all done.
She's so long comin' till she worries my mind,
Seems to be late, but she's just on time.

It keeps me always in a move an' strain,
Tryin' to be ready for the Gospel train.
Ever now an' then, either day or night,
I examine my tickit to see if I'm right.
If the Son grant my ticket the Holy Ghost sign,
Then there is no way to be left behind.

There's a great deal of talk 'bout the Judgment Day,
You have no time for to trifle away.
I'll tell you one thing certain an' sho',
Judgment Day's comin' when you don't know.
I hope to be ready when I'm called to go,
If anything's lackin', Lawd, let me know.

Shouting Songs and Songs of Triumph

# I'M RUNNIN' ON

# I'M RUNNIN' ON

*I'm runnin' on, I'm runnin' on,*
*I done left this world behind;*
*I done crossed the separatin' line,*
*I done left this world behind.*

So, free, so free—
I done left this world behind;
I done crossed the separatin' line,
An' I've left this world behind.

Ain't you glad?  Ain't you glad?
I done left this world behind;
I done crossed the separatin' line,
An' I've left this world behind.

Pressin' on, pressin' on—
I done left this world behind;
I done crossed the separatin' line,
An' I've left this world behind.

Won't turn back, won't turn back—
I done left this world behind;
I done crossed the separatin' line,
An' I've left this world behind.

Good-bye!  Good bye!
I done left this world behind;
I done crossed the separatin' line,
An' I've left this world behind.

# I FOUND JESUS OVER IN ZION

MM(♩=100)

I found Je — — sus — o - ver in Zi - yun an' He's

mine, mine, mine, mine mine — — — I found

Je — sus o — ver in Zi — yun an' He's mine, mine, mine, mine - mine.

# I FOUND JESUS OVER IN ZION

I found Jesus over in Ziyun,
An' He's mine, mine, mine, mine, mine;
I found Jesus over in Ziyun,
An He's mine, mine, mine, mine, mine.

I found the Holy Ghost over in Ziyun,
An' He's mine, mine, mine, mine, mine;
I found the Holy Ghost over in Ziyun,
An' He's mine, mine, mine, mine, mine.

I got sanctified over in Ziyun,
An' it's mine, mine, mine, mine, mine;
I got sanctified over in Ziyun,
An' it's mine, mine, mine, mine, mine.

I got baptized over in Ziyun,
An' I'm saved, saved, saved, saved, saved;
I got baptized over in Ziyun,
An' I'm saved, saved, saved, saved, saved.

He's mah Savior, He's mah Savior—
Oh, He's mine, mine, mine, mine, mine.
He's mah Savior, He's mah Savior—
Yes, He's mine, mine, mine, mine, mine.

# I GOT A HIDIN' PLACE

CHORUS

I got a hi—din' place—— In de Word of God

I got a hi——din' place— The ship she stop In de

LEADER

mid—dle of de sea, Jo-nah cried out—— Lawd have

CHORUS

mer—cy is it me, Throw me ov-er boad I got a hi—din' place-

—— Throw me ov er boa'd I got a hi—— din' place——

# I GOT A HIDIN' PLACE

*I got a hidin' place—*
*In de Word of God,*
*I got a hidin' place.*

he ship she stop
a de middle of de sea,
nah cried out—
awd have mercy, is it me?
  Throw me overboa'd.
got a hidin' place,
  Throw me overboa'd,
got a hidin' place.
got a hidin' place—
  In de Word of God,
got a hidin' place.

Yonder what's the matter
hat de ship don't go;
here's too many liyuhs
ittin' on boa'd.
  Throw 'em overboa'd.
got a hidin' place,
  Throw 'em overboa'd,
got a hidin' place.
got a hidin' place—
  In de Word of God,
got a hidin' place.

Wonder what's the matter
That de ship won't go;
There's too many hypocrits
Gittin' on boa'd.
  Well you cain't hide now.
I got a hidin' place,
  Well you cain't hide now,
I got a hidin' place.
I got a hidin' place—
  In de Word of God,
I got a hidin' place.

Tell that watchman
That he cain't hide;
If he hasn't got de Holy Ghost
He cain't ride.
  Get de Holy Ghost.
I got a hidin' place,
  Get de Holy Ghost,
I got a hidin' place.
I got a hidin' place—
  In de Word of God,
I got a hidin' place.

There's too many people
Like Jonah today;
God sends'um out
An' they will not obey.
  Won't you help me Lawd?
I got a hidin' place,
  Won't you help me Lawd?
I got a hidin' place.
I got a hidin' place—
  In de Word of God,
I got a hidin' place.

If you wawnta go to heabum,
Like anybody else;
Treat yo' neighbuh
Like you treat yo'self.
  Treat yo' neighbuh right.
I got a hidin' place,
  Treat yo' neighbuh right,
I got a hidin' place.
I got a hidin' place—
  Roun' de throne of God,
I got a hidin' place.

Well, when I git to heabum
Gonna sing an' shout;
There's nobody there
Gonna put me out.
  Well in Canaan land.
I got a hidin' place,
  Well in Canaan land,
I got a hidin' place.
I got a hidin' place—
  Roun' de throne of God,
I got a hidin' place.

# NO CONDEMNATION IN MY SOUL

CHORUS (Not too fast)

I feel all right —— no con-dem—na—tion, Feel all right

no con—dem—na-tion, Well I feel all right— no con-dem-na-tion

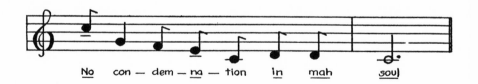

No con — dem — na — tion in mah soul

# NO CONDEMNATION IN MY SOUL

*I feel all right, no condemnation—*
*Feel all right, no condemnation—*
*Well, I feel all right, no condemnation—*
*No condemnation in mah soul.*

I been bawn of God, no condemnation—
Bawn of God, no condemnation—
I been bawn of God, no condemnation—
No condemnation in mah soul.

I been baptized, no condemnation—
Been baptized, no condemnation—
Well, I been baptized, no condemnation—
No condemnation in mah soul.

I been sanctified, no condemnation—
Sanctified, no condemnation—
I been sanctified, no condemnation—
No condemnation in mah soul.

Got the Holy Ghost, no condemnation—
Holy Ghost, no condemnation—
Got the Holy Ghost, no condemnation—
No condemnation in mah soul.

When I see my Lawd, no condemnation—
See my Lawd, no condemnation—
When I see my Lawd, no condemnation—
No condemnation in mah soul.

NOTE—This song, together with many others of its type, is a great shouting song. Constant repetitions and vigorous rhythm give full opportunity for spending freely of emotion.

# WHEN JESUS COMES

When  Je —— sus    comes  He'll  out—shine thuh  Sun —a

Out —— shine——thuh   Sun —— a    out—shine thuh Sun ———— a

When   Je —— sus     comes He'll   Out — shine  thuh Sun,  Look—a

way     be ——   yond    they ——— moon. ———

## WHEN JESUS COMES

When Jesus comes,
He'll outshine thuh sun,
   Outshine thuh sun,
   Outshine thuh sun,
When Jesus comes,
He'll outshine thuh sun,
Look away beyond they moon.

We'll shout Hallelujah!
   When Jesus comes,
   When Jesus comes,
   When Jesus comes.
We'll shout Hallelujah!
   When Jesus comes,
Look away beyond they moon.

We'll sing Hosyannah—
   When Jesus comes,
   When Jesus comes,
   When Jesus comes.
We'll sing Hosyannah—
   When Jesus comes,
Look away beyond they moon.

They'll be no mo' sorruh in
   Sweet Beuly Land,
   Sweet Beuly Land,
   Sweet Beuly Land.
They'll be no mo' sorruh in
   Sweet Beuly Land,
Look away beyond they moon.

If you wawn-tuh see King Jesus,
   Keep prayin' awn,
   Keep prayin' awn,
   Keep prayin' awn.
If you wawn-tuh see King Jesus,
   Keep prayin' awn,
Look away beyond they moon.

Gonna meet my dear Mother in
   Sweet Beuly Land,
   Sweet Beuly Land,
   Sweet Beuly Land.
Gonna meet my dear Mother in
   Sweet Beuly Land,
Look away beyond they moon.

Gonna meet my dear Sister in
   Sweet Beuly Land,
   Sweet Beuly Land,
   Sweet Beuly Land.
Gonna meet my dear Sister in
   Sweet Beuly Land,
Look away beyond they moon.

Gonna meet all my frien's in
   Sweet Beuly Land,
   Sweet Beuly Land,
   Sweet Beuly Land.
Gonna meet all my frien's in
   Sweet Beuly Land,
Look away beyond they moon.

# HE'S THE LILY OF THE VALLEY

He's the Li—ly of the val—ley He's mah Lawd. He's the

white Rose of Shar—on He's—mah Lawd

He's the Great Phy—si—cian He's mah Lawd. He

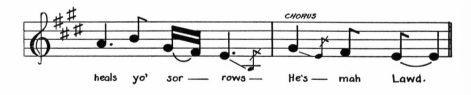

heals yo' sor—rows— He's—mah Lawd.

# HE'S THE LILY OF THE VALLEY

*He's the Lily of the valley,*
*He's mah Lawd;*
*He's the white Rose of Sharon,*
*He's mah Lawd.*

He's the Great Physician,
    He's mah Lawd;
He heals yo' sorrows,
    He's mah Lawd.

He's the Alpha and Omego, the beginning and the end,
    He's mah Lawd;
He's the Shepherd of the flock, the door to enter in,
    He's mah Lawd.

He's the Lord that was an' is to come,
    He's mah Lawd;
He's the Rock the church is built upon,
    He's mah Lawd.

He's the Bread of Heaven, the Truth, the Way,
    He's mah Lawd;
He's the Light that shines to a perfect day,
    He's mah Lawd.

He's the Balm of Gilead, the Great Physician,
    He's mah Lawd;
By His stripes we are healed of all diseases,
    He's mah Lawd.

I'll tell the nations, both great an' small,
    He's mah Lawd;
The blood of Jesus saves us all,
    He's mah Lawd.

# I GOT A KEY TO THE KINGDOM

# I GOT A KEY TO THE KINGDOM

*I got a Key to thuh Kingdom,*
*I got a Key. Oh, yes, I have-a now.*
*I got a Key to thuh Kingdom,*
*An' the worl' can't do me no harm.*

Oh, If you know you're livin' right,
Servin' God both night an' day;
An' when you go down awn yo' knees,
God will hear ev'ry word you say. Singin'
I got a Key, *etc.*

Oh! When you know you're livin' right,
An' you're doing nobody no wrong;
Jus' call up Central in Heaven,
Tell Jesus to come to thuh phone. Singin'
I got a Key, *etc.*

Oh! Git yo' trumpet, Gabul,
An' come down awn thuh sea;
Now don't you sound yo' trumpet
'Tel you git ordahs frum me. Singin'
I got a Key, *etc.*

Now when I git to Heaven,
I want you to be tha', too;
An' when I hollah, Hallelujah!
I want you to hollah, too. Singin'
I got a Key, *etc.*

They took ole Paul an' Silus,
An' put 'em in a jail below;
The angel come down frum Heaven,
An' they tell me he unlocked thuh do'. Singin'
I got a Key, *etc.*

Prayer is the Key to the Kingdom,
An' Faith unlocks thuh do'. Oh! Yes,
If you got a Key to Heaven,
You can pray ev'rywhere you go. Singin'
I got a Key, *etc.*

# LET THE CHURCH ROLL ON

Let the church roll    on      my     Lawd, Let the church roll

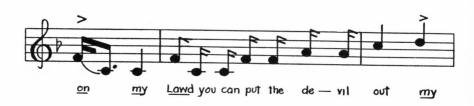

on      my    Lawd you can put the    de — vil    out      my

Lawd Let the    church roll    on ——————

## LET THE CHURCH ROLL ON

Let the church roll on, my Lawd,
Let the church roll on, my Lawd.
You can put the devil out, my Lawd,
   Let the church roll on.

If tha's preachers in the church, my Lawd,
An' they're not livin' right, my Lawd;
Jes' turn the preachers out, my Lawd,
   An' let the church roll on.

If tha's members in the church, my Lawd,
An' they're not livin' right, my Lawd;
You can put the members out, my Lawd,
   An' let the church roll on.

If tha's liars in the church, my Lawd,
An' they're not livin' right, my Lawd;
You can put the liars out, my Lawd,
   An' let the church roll on.

If tha's sinnuhs in the church, my Lawd,
An' they're not livin' right, my Lawd,
Jes' put the sinnuhs out, my Lawd,
   An let the church roll on.

NOTE—This is a favorite shouting song.

A CATALOGUE OF SELECTED DOVER BOOKS
IN ALL FIELDS OF INTEREST

# A CATALOGUE OF SELECTED DOVER BOOKS
## IN ALL FIELDS OF INTEREST

WHAT IS SCIENCE?, *N. Campbell*
The role of experiment and measurement, the function of mathematics, the nature of scientific laws, the difference between laws and theories, the limitations of science, and many similarly provocative topics are treated clearly and without technicalities by an eminent scientist. "Still an excellent introduction to scientific philosophy," H. Margenau in *Physics Today*. "A first-rate primer . . . deserves a wide audience," *Scientific American*. 192pp. 5⅜ x 8.
S43    Paperbound $1.25

THE NATURE OF LIGHT AND COLOUR IN THE OPEN AIR, *M. Minnaert*
Why are shadows sometimes blue, sometimes green, or other colors depending on the light and surroundings? What causes mirages? Why do multiple suns and moons appear in the sky? Professor Minnaert explains these unusual phenomena and hundreds of others in simple, easy-to-understand terms based on optical laws and the properties of light and color. No mathematics is required but artists, scientists, students, and everyone fascinated by these "tricks" of nature will find thousands of useful and amazing pieces of information. Hundreds of observational experiments are suggested which require no special equipment. 200 illustrations; 42 photos. xvi + 362pp. 5⅜ x 8.
T196    Paperbound $2.00

THE STRANGE STORY OF THE QUANTUM, AN ACCOUNT FOR THE GENERAL READER OF THE GROWTH OF IDEAS UNDERLYING OUR PRESENT ATOMIC KNOWLEDGE, *B. Hoffmann*
Presents lucidly and expertly, with barest amount of mathematics, the problems and theories which led to modern quantum physics. Dr. Hoffmann begins with the closing years of the 19th century, when certain trifling discrepancies were noticed, and with illuminating analogies and examples takes you through the brilliant concepts of Planck, Einstein, Pauli, Broglie, Bohr, Schroedinger, Heisenberg, Dirac, Sommerfeld, Feynman, etc. This edition includes a new, long postscript carrying the story through 1958. "Of the books attempting an account of the history and contents of our modern atomic physics which have come to my attention, this is the best," H. Margenau, Yale University, in *American Journal of Physics*. 32 tables and line illustrations. Index. 275pp. 5⅜ x 8.    T518    Paperbound $2.00

GREAT IDEAS OF MODERN MATHEMATICS: THEIR NATURE AND USE, *Jagjit Singh*
Reader with only high school math will understand main mathematical ideas of modern physics, astronomy, genetics, psychology, evolution, etc. better than many who use them as tools, but comprehend little of their basic structure. Author uses his wide knowledge of non-mathematical fields in brilliant exposition of differential equations, matrices, group theory, logic, statistics, problems of mathematical foundations, imaginary numbers, vectors, etc. Original publication. 2 appendixes. 2 indexes. 65 ills. 322pp. 5⅜ x 8.
T587    Paperbound $2.00

A SHORT ACCOUNT OF THE HISTORY OF MATHEMATICS,
*W. W. Rouse Ball*
Last previous edition (1908) hailed by mathematicians and laymen for lucid overview of math as living science, for understandable presentation of individual contributions of great mathematicians. Treats lives, discoveries of every important school and figure from Egypt, Phoenicia to late nineteenth century. Greek schools of Ionia, Cyzicus, Alexandria, Byzantium, Pythagoras; primitive arithmetic; Middle Ages and Renaissance, including European and Asiatic contributions; modern math of Descartes, Pascal, Wallis, Huygens, Newton, Euler, Lambert, Laplace, scores more. More emphasis on historical development, exposition of ideas than other books on subject. Non-technical, readable text can be followed with no more preparation than high-school algebra. Index. 544pp. 5⅜ x 8.                                           Paperbound $2.25

GREAT IDEAS AND THEORIES OF MODERN COSMOLOGY, *Jagjit Singh*
Companion volume to author's popular "Great Ideas of Modern Mathematics" (Dover, $2.00). The best non-technical survey of post-Einstein attempts to answer perhaps unanswerable questions of origin, age of Universe, possibility of life on other worlds, etc. Fundamental theories of cosmology and cosmogony recounted, explained, evaluated in light of most recent data: Einstein's concepts of relativity, space-time; Milne's a priori world-system; astrophysical theories of Jeans, Eddington; Hoyle's "continuous creation;" contributions of dozens more scientists. A faithful, comprehensive critical summary of complex material presented in an extremely well-written text intended for laymen. Original publication. Index. xii + 276pp. 5⅜ x 8½.       Paperbound $2.00

THE RESTLESS UNIVERSE, *Max Born*
A remarkably lucid account by a Nobel Laureate of recent theories of wave mechanics, behavior of gases, electrons and ions, waves and particles, electronic structure of the atom, nuclear physics, and similar topics. "Much more thorough and deeper than most attempts . . . easy and delightful," *Chemical and Engineering News*. Special feature: 7 animated sequences of 60 figures each showing such phenomena as gas molecules in motion, the scattering of alpha particles, etc. 11 full-page plates of photographs. Total of nearly 600 illustrations. 351pp. 6⅛ x 9¼.                                         Paperbound $2.00

PLANETS, STARS AND GALAXIES: DESCRIPTIVE ASTRONOMY FOR BEGINNERS,
*A. E. Fanning*
What causes the progression of the seasons? Phases of the moon? The Aurora Borealis? How much does the sun weigh? What are the chances of life on our sister planets? Absorbing introduction to astronomy, incorporating the latest discoveries and theories: the solar wind, the surface temperature of Venus, the pock-marked face of Mars, quasars, and much more. Places you on the frontiers of one of the most vital sciences of our time. Revised (1966). Introduction by Donald H. Menzel, Harvard University. References. Index. 45 illustrations. 189pp. 5¼ x 8¼.                                         Paperbound $1.50

GREAT IDEAS IN INFORMATION THEORY, LANGUAGE AND CYBERNETICS,
*Jagjit Singh*
Non-mathematical, but profound study of information, language, the codes used by men and machines to communicate, the principles of analog and digital computers, work of McCulloch, Pitts, von Neumann, Turing, and Uttley, correspondences between intricate mechanical network of "thinking machines" and more intricate neurophysiological mechanism of human brain. Indexes. 118 figures. 50 tables. ix + 338pp. 5⅜ x 8½.       Paperbound $2.00

THE MUSIC OF THE SPHERES: THE MATERIAL UNIVERSE — FROM ATOM TO QUASAR, SIMPLY EXPLAINED, *Guy Murchie*
Vast compendium of fact, modern concept and theory, observed and calculated data, historical background guides intelligent layman through the material universe. Brilliant exposition of earth's construction, explanations for moon's craters, atmospheric components of Venus and Mars (with data from recent fly-by's), sun spots, sequences of star birth and death, neighboring galaxies, contributions of Galileo, Tycho Brahe, Kepler, etc.; and (Vol. 2) construction of the atom (describing newly discovered sigma and xi subatomic particles), theories of sound, color and light, space and time, including relativity theory, quantum theory, wave theory, probability theory, work of Newton, Maxwell, Faraday, Einstein, de Broglie, etc. "Best presentation yet offered to the intelligent general reader," *Saturday Review*. Revised (1967). Index. 319 illustrations by the author. Total of xx + 644pp. 5⅜ x 8½.
Vol. 1 Paperbound $2.00, Vol. 2 Paperbound $2.00,
The set $4.00

FOUR LECTURES ON RELATIVITY AND SPACE, *Charles Proteus Steinmetz*
Lecture series, given by great mathematician and electrical engineer, generally considered one of the best popular-level expositions of special and general relativity theories and related questions. Steinmetz translates complex mathematical reasoning into language accessible to laymen through analogy, example and comparison. Among topics covered are relativity of motion, location, time; of mass; acceleration; 4-dimensional time-space; geometry of the gravitational field; curvature and bending of space; non-Euclidean geometry. Index. 40 illustrations. x + 142pp. 5⅜ x 8½.
Paperbound $1.35

HOW TO KNOW THE WILD FLOWERS, *Mrs. William Starr Dana*
Classic nature book that has introduced thousands to wonders of American wild flowers. Color-season principle of organization is easy to use, even by those with no botanical training, and the genial, refreshing discussions of history, folklore, uses of over 1,000 native and escape flowers, foliage plants are informative as well as fun to read. Over 170 full-page plates, collected from several editions, may be colored in to make permanent records of finds. Revised to conform with 1950 edition of Gray's Manual of Botany. xlii + 438pp. 5⅜ x 8½.
Paperbound $2.00

MANUAL OF THE TREES OF NORTH AMERICA, *Charles Sprague Sargent*
Still unsurpassed as most comprehensive, reliable study of North American tree characteristics, precise locations and distribution. By dean of American dendrologists. Every tree native to U.S., Canada, Alaska; 185 genera, 717 species, described in detail—leaves, flowers, fruit, winterbuds, bark, wood, growth habits, etc. plus discussion of varieties and local variants, immaturity variations. Over 100 keys, including unusual 11-page analytical key to genera, aid in identification. 783 clear illustrations of flowers, fruit, leaves. An unmatched permanent reference work for all nature lovers. Second enlarged (1926) edition. Synopsis of families. Analytical key to genera. Glossary of technical terms. Index. 783 illustrations, 1 map. Total of 982pp. 5⅜ x 8.
Vol. 1 Paperbound $2.25, Vol. 2 Paperbound $2.25,
The set $4.50

IT'S FUN TO MAKE THINGS FROM SCRAP MATERIALS,
*Evelyn Glantz Hershoff*
What use are empty spools, tin cans, bottle tops? What can be made from
rubber bands, clothes pins, paper clips, and buttons? This book provides
simply worded instructions and large diagrams showing you how to make
cookie cutters, toy trucks, paper turkeys, Halloween masks, telephone sets,
aprons, linoleum block- and spatter prints — in all 399 projects! Many are easy
enough for young children to figure out for themselves; some challenging
enough to entertain adults; all are remarkably ingenious ways to make things
from materials that cost pennies or less! Formerly "Scrap Fun for Everyone."
Index. 214 illustrations. 373pp. 5⅜ x 8½.                    Paperbound $1.50

SYMBOLIC LOGIC and THE GAME OF LOGIC, *Lewis Carroll*
"Symbolic Logic" is not concerned with modern symbolic logic, but is instead
a collection of over 380 problems posed with charm and imagination, using
the syllogism and a fascinating diagrammatic method of drawing conclusions.
In "The Game of Logic" Carroll's whimsical imagination devises a logical game
played with 2 diagrams and counters (included) to manipulate hundreds of
tricky syllogisms. The final section, "Hit or Miss" is a lagniappe of 101 additional puzzles in the delightful Carroll manner. Until this reprint edition,
both of these books were rarities costing up to $15 each. Symbolic Logic:
Index. xxxi + 199pp. The Game of Logic: 96pp. 2 vols. bound as one. 5⅜ x 8.
                                                           Paperbound $2.00

MATHEMATICAL PUZZLES OF SAM LOYD, PART I
*selected and edited by M. Gardner*
Choice puzzles by the greatest American puzzle creator and innovator. Selected
from his famous collection, "Cyclopedia of Puzzles," they retain the unique
style and historical flavor of the originals. There are posers based on arithmetic,
algebra, probability, game theory, route tracing, topology, counter and sliding
block, operations research, geometrical dissection. Includes the famous "14-15"
puzzle which was a national craze, and his "Horse of a Different Color" which
sold millions of copies. 117 of his most ingenious puzzles in all. 120 line
drawings and diagrams. Solutions. Selected references. xx + 167pp. 5⅜ x 8.
                                                           Paperbound $1.00

STRING FIGURES AND HOW TO MAKE THEM, *Caroline Furness Jayne*
107 string figures plus variations selected from the best primitive and modern
examples developed by Navajo, Apache, pygmies of Africa, Eskimo, in Europe,
Australia, China, etc. The most readily understandable, easy-to-follow book in
English on perennially popular recreation. Crystal-clear exposition; step-by-
step diagrams. Everyone from kindergarten children to adults looking for
unusual diversion will be endlessly amused. Index. Bibliography. Introduction
by A. C. Haddon. 17 full-page plates, 960 illustrations. xxiii + 401pp. 5⅜ x 8½.
                                                           Paperbound $2.00

PAPER FOLDING FOR BEGINNERS, *W. D. Murray and F. J. Rigney*
A delightful introduction to the varied and entertaining Japanese art of
origami (paper folding), with a full, crystal-clear text that anticipates every
difficulty; over 275 clearly labeled diagrams of all important stages in creation.
You get results at each stage, since complex figures are logically developed
from simpler ones. 43 different pieces are explained: sailboats, frogs, roosters,
etc. 6 photographic plates. 279 diagrams. 95pp. 5⅝ x 8⅜. Paperbound $1.00

PRINCIPLES OF ART HISTORY,
*H. Wölfflin*
Analyzing such terms as "baroque," "classic," "neoclassic," "primitive,"
"picturesque," and 164 different works by artists like Botticelli, van Cleve,
Dürer, Hobbema, Holbein, Hals, Rembrandt, Titian, Brueghel, Vermeer, and
many others, the author establishes the classifications of art history and style
on a firm, concrete basis. This classic of art criticism shows what really
occurred between the 14th-century primitives and the sophistication of the
18th century in terms of basic attitudes and philosophies. "A remarkable
lesson in the art of seeing," *Sat. Rev. of Literature.* Translated from the 7th
German edition. 150 illustrations. 254pp. 6⅛ x 9¼.          Paperbound $2.00

PRIMITIVE ART,
*Franz Boas*
This authoritative and exhaustive work by a great American anthropologist
covers the entire gamut of primitive art. Pottery, leatherwork, metal work,
stone work, wood, basketry, are treated in detail. Theories of primitive art,
historical depth in art history, technical virtuosity, unconscious levels of pat-
terning, symbolism, styles, literature, music, dance, etc. A must book for the
interested layman, the anthropologist, artist, handicrafter (hundreds of unusual motifs), and the historian. Over 900 illustrations (50 ceramic vessels,
12 totem poles, etc.). 376pp. 5⅜ x 8.          Paperbound $2.25

THE GENTLEMAN AND CABINET MAKER'S DIRECTOR,
*Thomas Chippendale*
A reprint of the 1762 catalogue of furniture designs that went on to influence
generations of English and Colonial and Early Republic American furniture
makers. The 200 plates, most of them full-page sized, show Chippendale's
designs for French (Louis XV), Gothic, and Chinese-manner chairs, sofas,
canopy and dome beds, cornices, chamber organs, cabinets, shaving tables,
commodes, picture frames, frets, candle stands, chimney pieces, decorations, etc.
The drawings are all elegant and highly detailed; many include construction
diagrams and elevations. A supplement of 24 photographs shows surviving
pieces of original and Chippendale-style pieces of furniture. Brief biography
of Chippendale by N. I. Bienenstock, editor of *Furniture World*. Reproduced
from the 1762 edition. 200 plates, plus 19 photographic plates. vi + 249pp.
9⅛ x 12¼.          Paperbound $3.50

AMERICAN ANTIQUE FURNITURE: A BOOK FOR AMATEURS,
*Edgar G. Miller, Jr.*
Standard introduction and practical guide to identification of valuable
American antique furniture. 2115 illustrations, mostly photographs taken by
the author in 148 private homes, are arranged in chronological order in exten-
sive chapters on chairs, sofas, chests, desks, bedsteads, mirrors, tables, clocks,
and other articles. Focus is on furniture accessible to the collector, including
simpler pieces and a larger than usual coverage of Empire style. Introductory
chapters identify structural elements characteristics of various styles, how to
avoid fakes, etc. "We are frequently asked to name some book on American
furniture that will meet the requirements of the novice collector, the beginning dealer, and . . . the general public. . . . We believe Mr. Miller's two
volumes more completely satisfy this specification than any other work,"
*Antiques.* Appendix. Index. Total of vi + 1106pp. 7⅞ x 10¾.
          Two volume set, paperbound $7.50

THE BAD CHILD'S BOOK OF BEASTS, MORE BEASTS FOR WORSE CHILDREN, and A MORAL ALPHABET, *H. Belloc*
Hardly and anthology of humorous verse has appeared in the last 50 years without at least a couple of these famous nonsense verses. But one must see the entire volumes — with all the delightful original illustrations by Sir Basil Blackwood — to appreciate fully Belloc's charming and witty verses that play so subacidly on the platitudes of life and morals that beset his day — and ours. A great humor classic. Three books in one. Total of 157pp. 5⅜ x 8.
Paperbound $1.00

THE DEVIL'S DICTIONARY, *Ambrose Bierce*
Sardonic and irreverent barbs puncturing the pomposities and absurdities of American politics, business, religion, literature, and arts, by the country's greatest satirist in the classic tradition. Epigrammatic as Shaw, piercing as Swift, American as Mark Twain, Will Rogers, and Fred Allen, Bierce will always remain the favorite of a small coterie of enthusiasts, and of writers and speakers whom he supplies with "some of the most gorgeous witticisms of the English language" (H. L. Mencken). Over 1000 entries in alphabetical order. 144pp. 5⅜ x 8.
Paperbound $1.00

THE COMPLETE NONSENSE OF EDWARD LEAR.
This is the only complete edition of this master of gentle madness available at a popular price. *A Book of Nonsense, Nonsense Songs, More Nonsense Songs and Stories* in their entirety with all the old favorites that have delighted children and adults for years. The Dong With A Luminous Nose, The Jumblies, The Owl and the Pussycat, and hundreds of other bits of wonderful nonsense. 214 limericks, 3 sets of Nonsense Botany, 5 Nonsense Alphabets, 546 drawings by Lear himself, and much more. 320pp. 5⅜ x 8.
Paperbound $1.00

THE WIT AND HUMOR OF OSCAR WILDE, *ed. by Alvin Redman*
Wilde at his most brilliant, in 1000 epigrams exposing weaknesses and hypocrisies of "civilized" society. Divided into 49 categories—sin, wealth, women, America, etc.—to aid writers, speakers. Includes excerpts from his trials, books, plays, criticism. Formerly "The Epigrams of Oscar Wilde." Introduction by Vyvyan Holland, Wilde's only living son. Introductory essay by editor. 260pp. 5⅜ x 8.
Paperbound $1.00

A CHILD'S PRIMER OF NATURAL HISTORY, *Oliver Herford*
Scarcely an anthology of whimsy and humor has appeared in the last 50 years without a contribution from Oliver Herford. Yet the works from which these examples are drawn have been almost impossible to obtain! Here at last are Herford's improbable definitions of a menagerie of familiar and weird animals, each verse illustrated by the author's own drawings. 24 drawings in 2 colors; 24 additional drawings. vii + 95pp. 6½ x 6.
Paperbound $1.00

THE BROWNIES: THEIR BOOK, *Palmer Cox*
The book that made the Brownies a household word. Generations of readers have enjoyed the antics, predicaments and adventures of these jovial sprites, who emerge from the forest at night to play or to come to the aid of a deserving human. Delightful illustrations by the author decorate nearly every page. 24 short verse tales with 266 illustrations. 155pp. 6⅝ x 9¼.
Paperbound $1.50

THE PRINCIPLES OF PSYCHOLOGY,
*William James*
The full long-course, unabridged, of one of the great classics of Western literature and science. Wonderfully lucid descriptions of human mental activity, the stream of thought, consciousness, time perception, memory, imagination, emotions, reason, abnormal phenomena, and similar topics. Original contributions are integrated with the work of such men as Berkeley, Binet, Mills, Darwin, Hume, Kant, Royce, Schopenhauer, Spinoza, Locke, Descartes, Galton, Wundt, Lotze, Herbart, Fechner, and scores of others. All contrasting interpretations of mental phenomena are examined in detail—introspective analysis, philosophical interpretation, and experimental research. "A classic," *Journal of Consulting Psychology.* "The main lines are as valid as ever," *Psychoanalytical Quarterly.* "Standard reading . . . a classic of interpretation," *Psychiatric Quarterly.* 94 illustrations. 1408pp. 5⅜ x 8.
Vol. 1 Paperbound $2.50, Vol. 2 Paperbound $2.50,
The set $5.00

VISUAL ILLUSIONS: THEIR CAUSES, CHARACTERISTICS AND APPLICATIONS,
*M. Luckiesh*
"Seeing is deceiving," asserts the author of this introduction to virtually every type of optical illusion known. The text both describes and explains the principles involved in color illusions, figure-ground, distance illusions, etc. 100 photographs, drawings and diagrams prove how easy it is to fool the sense: circles that aren't round, parallel lines that seem to bend, stationary figures that seem to move as you stare at them — illustration after illustration strains our credulity at what we see. Fascinating book from many points of view, from applications for artists, in camouflage, etc. to the psychology of vision. New introduction by William Ittleson, Dept. of Psychology, Queens College. Index. Bibliography. xxi + 252pp. 5⅜ x 8½. Paperbound $1.50

FADS AND FALLACIES IN THE NAME OF SCIENCE,
*Martin Gardner*
This is the standard account of various cults, quack systems, and delusions which have masqueraded as science: hollow earth fanatics. Reich and orgone sex energy, dianetics, Atlantis, multiple moons, Forteanism, flying saucers, medical fallacies like iridiagnosis, zone therapy, etc. A new chapter has been added on Bridey Murphy, psionics, and other recent manifestations in this field. This is a fair, reasoned appraisal of eccentric theory which provides excellent inoculation against cleverly masked nonsense. "Should be read by everyone, scientist and non-scientist alike," R. T. Birge, Prof. Emeritus of Physics, Univ. of California; Former President, American Physical Society. Index. x + 365pp. 5⅜ x 8. Paperbound $1.85

ILLUSIONS AND DELUSIONS OF THE SUPERNATURAL AND THE OCCULT,
*D. H. Rawcliffe*
Holds up to rational examination hundreds of persistent delusions including crystal gazing, automatic writing, table turning, mediumistic trances, mental healing, stigmata, lycanthropy, live burial, the Indian Rope Trick, spiritualism, dowsing, telepathy, clairvoyance, ghosts, ESP, etc. The author explains and exposes the mental and physical deceptions involved, making this not only an exposé of supernatural phenomena, but a valuable exposition of characteristic types of abnormal psychology. Originally titled "The Psychology of the Occult." 14 illustrations. Index. 551pp. 5⅜ x 8. Paperbound $2.25

THE WONDERFUL WIZARD OF OZ, *L. F. Baum*
All the original W. W. Denslow illustrations in full color—as much a part of "The Wizard" as Tenniel's drawings are of "Alice in Wonderland." "The Wizard" is still America's best-loved fairy tale, in which, as the author expresses it, "The wonderment and joy are retained and the heartaches and nightmares left out." Now today's young readers can enjoy every word and wonderful picture of the original book. New introduction by Martin Gardner. A Baum bibliography. 23 full-page color plates. viii + 268pp. 5⅜ x 8.
T691 Paperbound $1.75

THE MARVELOUS LAND OF OZ, *L. F. Baum*
This is the equally enchanting sequel to the "Wizard," continuing the adventures of the Scarecrow and the Tin Woodman. The hero this time is a little boy named Tip, and all the delightful Oz magic is still present. This is the Oz book with the Animated Saw-Horse, the Woggle-Bug, and Jack Pumpkinhead. All the original John R. Neill illustrations, 10 in full color. 287pp. 5⅜ x 8.
T692 Paperbound $1.50

ALICE'S ADVENTURES UNDER GROUND, *Lewis Carroll*
The original *Alice in Wonderland*, hand-lettered and illustrated by Carroll himself, and originally presented as a Christmas gift to a child-friend. Adults as well as children will enjoy this charming volume, reproduced faithfully in this Dover edition. While the story is essentially the same, there are slight changes, and Carroll's spritely drawings present an intriguing alternative to the famous Tenniel illustrations. One of the most popular books in Dover's catalogue. Introduction by Martin Gardner. 38 illustrations. 128pp. 5⅜ x 8½.
T1482 Paperbound $1.00

THE NURSERY "ALICE," *Lewis Carroll*
While most of us consider *Alice in Wonderland* a story for children of all ages, Carroll himself felt it was beyond younger children. He therefore provided this simplified version, illustrated with the famous Tenniel drawings enlarged and colored in delicate tints, for children aged "from Nought to Five." Dover's edition of this now rare classic is a faithful copy of the 1889 printing, including 20 illustrations by Tenniel, and front and back covers reproduced in full color. Introduction by Martin Gardner. xxiii + 67pp. 6⅛ x 9¼.
T1610 Paperbound $1.75

THE STORY OF KING ARTHUR AND HIS KNIGHTS, *Howard Pyle*
A fast-paced, exciting retelling of the best known Arthurian legends for young readers by one of America's best story tellers and illustrators. The sword Excalibur, wooing of Guinevere, Merlin and his downfall, adventures of Sir Pellias and Gawaine, and others. The pen and ink illustrations are vividly imagined and wonderfully drawn. 41 illustrations. xviii + 313pp. 6⅛ x 9¼.
T1445 Paperbound $1.75

*Prices subject to change without notice.*

Available at your book dealer or write for free catalogue to Dept. Adsci, Dover Publications, Inc., 180 Varick St., N.Y., N.Y. 10014. Dover publishes more than 150 books each year on science, elementary and advanced mathematics, biology, music, art, literary history, social sciences and other areas.